GW00362740

The
ROYAL HORTICULTURAL SOCIETY
Diary 1996

The
Language of Flowers

FRANCES LINCOLN

Frances Lincoln Limited
4 Torriano Mews
Torriano Avenue
London NW5 2RZ

The Royal Horticultural Society Diary 1996
Copyright © Frances Lincoln Limited 1995
Illustrations copyright © The Royal Horticultural Society 1995

Astronomical information reproduced, with permission, from data supplied by
HM Nautical Almanac Office, copyright © Particle Physics and Astronomy Research Council

Design by David Fordham

All rights reserved.
No part of this publication may be reproduced, stored in a retrieval system or transmitted, in any
form, or by any means, electronic, mechanical, photocopying, recording or otherwise, without
either the prior permission in writing from the publishers or a licence permitting restricted
copying. In the United Kingdom such licences are issued by the Copyright Licensing Agency,
90 Tottenham Court Road, London W1P 9HE.

British Library cataloguing-in-publication data.
A catalogue record for this book is available from the British Library.

ISBN 0-7112-0832-8

Typeset by SX Composing

Printed in Hong Kong

First Frances Lincoln edition: July 1995

RHS FLOWER SHOWS 1996

ALL SHOWS FEATURE a wide range of floral exhibits staged by the nursery trade, with associated
competitions reflecting seasonal changes, and horticultural sundries.

WITH THE EXCEPTION of the shows at Harrogate, Malvern, Chelsea, Birmingham, Hampton Court
and Wisley, all RHS Flower Shows will be held in one or both of the Society's Horticultural Halls
in Greycoat Street and Vincent Square, Westminster, London SW1.

THE DATES ARE CORRECT at time of going to press. Any amendments or alterations will be notified
in the Society's journal, *The Garden*. Up-to-date information on the Society's Flower Shows is
available on the RHS 24-hour information line, 0171 828 1744.

YEAR PLANNER

1996

January
M	T	W	T	F	S	S
1	2	3	4	5	6	7
8	9	10	11	12	13	14
15	16	17	18	19	20	21
22	23	24	25	26	27	28
29	30	31				

February
M	T	W	T	F	S	S
			1	2	3	4
5	6	7	8	9	10	11
12	13	14	15	16	17	18
19	20	21	22	23	24	25
26	27	28	29			

March
M	T	W	T	F	S	S
				1	2	3
4	5	6	7	8	9	10
11	12	13	14	15	16	17
18	19	20	21	22	23	24
25	26	27	28	29	30	31

April
M	T	W	T	F	S	S
1	2	3	4	5	6	7
8	9	10	11	12	13	14
15	16	17	18	19	20	21
22	23	24	25	26	27	28
29	30					

May
M	T	W	T	F	S	S
		1	2	3	4	5
6	7	8	9	10	11	12
13	14	15	16	17	18	19
20	21	22	23	24	25	26
27	28	29	30	31		

June
M	T	W	T	F	S	S
					1	2
3	4	5	6	7	8	9
10	11	12	13	14	15	16
17	18	19	20	21	22	23
24	25	26	27	28	29	30

July
M	T	W	T	F	S	S
1	2	3	4	5	6	7
8	9	10	11	12	13	14
15	16	17	18	19	20	21
22	23	24	25	26	27	28
29	30	31				

August
M	T	W	T	F	S	S
			1	2	3	4
5	6	7	8	9	10	11
12	13	14	15	16	17	18
19	20	21	22	23	24	25
26	27	28	29	30	31	

September
M	T	W	T	F	S	S
						1
2	3	4	5	6	7	8
9	10	11	12	13	14	15
16	17	18	19	20	21	22
23	24	25	26	27	28	29
30						

October
M	T	W	T	F	S	S
	1	2	3	4	5	6
7	8	9	10	11	12	13
14	15	16	17	18	19	20
21	22	23	24	25	26	27
28	29	30	31			

November
M	T	W	T	F	S	S
				1	2	3
4	5	6	7	8	9	10
11	12	13	14	15	16	17
18	19	20	21	22	23	24
25	26	27	28	29	30	

December
M	T	W	T	F	S	S
						1
2	3	4	5	6	7	8
9	10	11	12	13	14	15
16	17	18	19	20	21	22
23	24	25	26	27	28	29
30	31					

1997

January
M	T	W	T	F	S	S
		1	2	3	4	5
6	7	8	9	10	11	12
13	14	15	16	17	18	19
20	21	22	23	24	25	26
27	28	29	30	31		

February
M	T	W	T	F	S	S
					1	2
3	4	5	6	7	8	9
10	11	12	13	14	15	16
17	18	19	20	21	22	23
24	25	26	27	28		

March
M	T	W	T	F	S	S
					1	2
3	4	5	6	7	8	9
10	11	12	13	14	15	16
17	18	19	20	21	22	23
24	25	26	27	28	29	30
31						

April
M	T	W	T	F	S	S
	1	2	3	4	5	6
7	8	9	10	11	12	13
14	15	16	17	18	19	20
21	22	23	24	25	26	27
28	29	30				

May
M	T	W	T	F	S	S
			1	2	3	4
5	6	7	8	9	10	11
12	13	14	15	16	17	18
19	20	21	22	23	24	25
26	27	28	29	30	31	

June
M	T	W	T	F	S	S
						1
2	3	4	5	6	7	8
9	10	11	12	13	14	15
16	17	18	19	20	21	22
23	24	25	26	27	28	29
30						

July
M	T	W	T	F	S	S
	1	2	3	4	5	6
7	8	9	10	11	12	13
14	15	16	17	18	19	20
21	22	23	24	25	26	27
28	29	30	31			

August
M	T	W	T	F	S	S
				1	2	3
4	5	6	7	8	9	10
11	12	13	14	15	16	17
18	19	20	21	22	23	24
25	26	27	28	29	30	31

September
M	T	W	T	F	S	S
1	2	3	4	5	6	7
8	9	10	11	12	13	14
15	16	17	18	19	20	21
22	23	24	25	26	27	28
29	30					

October
M	T	W	T	F	S	S
		1	2	3	4	5
6	7	8	9	10	11	12
13	14	15	16	17	18	19
20	21	22	23	24	25	26
27	28	29	30	31		

November
M	T	W	T	F	S	S
					1	2
3	4	5	6	7	8	9
10	11	12	13	14	15	16
17	18	19	20	21	22	23
24	25	26	27	28	29	30

December
M	T	W	T	F	S	S
1	2	3	4	5	6	7
8	9	10	11	12	13	14
15	16	17	18	19	20	21
22	23	24	25	26	27	28
29	30	31				

○ Full Moon
◑ First Quarter
● New Moon
◐ Last Quarter

The Language of Flowers

T HE LANGUAGE OF FLOWERS first appeared in recognizable form in 1818, in *Le Langage des fleurs* by 'Charlotte de la Tour' (the pseudonym of Louise Cortambert). This little volume gave 313 messages that could be conveyed by presenting a flower, for the most part messages of love, of supplication, or of the refusal of advances. Some indicated a psychological state ('Patience', 'Voluptuousness', 'Frigidity'), while others gave specific instructions or responses ('My regrets follow you to the grave', 'Better to die than lose one's innocence'). Some meanings were suggested by classical mythology, narcissus indicating 'Egoism', for example; others came from the French vernacular names of the plants (*clandestine*, the French common name of *Leonurus cardiaca*, became 'Secrecy', a meaning that did not make much sense in England, where the common name of the plant was motherwort).

The language of flowers quickly became a popular nineteenth-century amusement – or perhaps 'amusements' would be a better word, for it appeared in different forms in French, German and English, and in each of those languages there were rival versions. By the 1830s, Charlotte de la Tour had been translated and adapted in England. Robert Tyas's *Sentiment of Flowers* (1853) and *Language of Flowers* (1869) became the best known adaptations. Like other English authors, Tyas applied traditional associations in favour of Charlotte de la Tour's when the French system conflicted with Shakespeare (thanks to Ophelia, rosemary stood for 'Remembrance', instead of 'Your presence revives me'). Associations with Roman Catholicism were removed, substituted by robust Protestant meanings (passion flowers changed their meaning from 'Faith' to 'Superstition'), and the sexual content of the French original was toned down (tuberoses ceased to mean 'Voluptuousness' and came to signify 'I have seen a lovely girl').

Some authors, most notably the 'poetical basket-weaver' Thomas Miller in his *Poetical Language of Flowers* (1847), drew up rival systems based on English literary allusion, but such attempts did not compete well with the system already established. Nor did a curious work, *The Catholic Language of Flowers* (1861) by 'The young ladies of Gumley House' (a Catholic convent), dedicated to Nicholas Wiseman, the Roman Catholic cardinal. After 1869, however, and the publication of John Ingram's *Flora Symbolica*, a new trend developed for books that were eclectic and comprehensive, giving multiple meanings where these existed.

By the 1850s, the language of flowers was crossing the Atlantic, but American versions had their own distinct character. They added entries for newly introduced exotics, especially greenhouse plants, which were given meanings before they received common names. They also introduced many transatlantic confusions: where English and American plant names differed, American compilers frequently cited the same plant under different names.

The publication of language of flowers books continued in America until the end of the century but declined in England after 1870, although the subject enjoyed a revival in popularity as a theme for picture postcards during the Edwardian era.

Given the possibilities for confusion resulting from the conflicting meanings to be found in different books, it is surprising that the language of flowers does not play a more significant role in nineteenth-century fiction, but its purpose was for amusement and this diary sets out to amuse today's readers with some of the conflicts of meaning that made up this rich and entertaining form of communication.

BRENT ELLIOT
The Royal Horticultural Society

Rosa indica

A hand-coloured stipple engraving by

PIERRE-JOSEPH REDOUTÉ from his *Les roses* (1817-24)

THE LANGUAGE OF FLOWERS DEVELOPED during the years when Redouté was publishing *Les roses*, and many different species and varieties of rose earned separate entries in the language. The rose on its own was almost universally given the meaning 'Beauty' until 1869, when John Ingram's *Flora Symbolica* identified it with 'Love' instead. Additional meanings included 'Genteel, pretty' and, in *The Catholic Language of Flowers* (1861), 'The sacred heart of Jesus'.

Crocus vernus

A hand-coloured stipple engraving of spring crocus by

PIERRE-JOSEPH REDOUTÉ from his *Les liliacées* (1802-16)

IN MOST LANGUAGE OF FLOWERS BOOKS, the crocus's association with early spring earned it the meaning of 'Youthfulness' or 'Youthful gladness'. Variants include 'Pleasures of hope', in Robert Tyas's *Language of Flowers* (1869); 'Smiles, cheerfulness', in some anonymous works; and 'Rashness' in *The Catholic Language of Flowers* (1861). In later works, the crocus sometimes borrowed the meaning of the saffron crocus, 'Abuse not'.

January 1996

New Year's Day Holiday, UK, Republic of Ireland, Canada, USA, Australia and New Zealand

MONDAY 1

Holiday, Scotland and New Zealand

TUESDAY 2

WEDNESDAY 3

THURSDAY 4

○ FRIDAY 5

Epiphany

SATURDAY 6

SUNDAY 7

January 1996

8 MONDAY

9 TUESDAY

10 WEDNESDAY

11 THURSDAY

12 FRIDAY

13 SATURDAY ◐

14 SUNDAY

Primula auricula

A hand-coloured stipple engraving of auriculas by

PIERRE-JOSEPH REDOUTÉ from his *Choix des plus belles fleurs* (1827-33)

THE AURICULA WAS ORIGINALLY MORE POPULAR in England than in France and thus was not included in Charlotte de la Tour's early and influential book, *Langage des fleurs* (1818). All English language of flowers books initially agreed on 'Painting' as the meaning, probably because interest in auriculas centred on their colours and edgings. *The Catholic Language of Flowers* (1861) redefined it as 'True happiness'.

Magnolia discolor

A hand-coloured stipple engraving by

P<small>IERRE</small>-J<small>OSEPH</small> R<small>EDOUTÉ</small> from Duhamel du Monceau's *Traité des arbres et arbustes* (1801-25)

T<small>HE MAGNOLIA ENTERED THE LANGUAGE OF FLOWERS</small> rather late; it appeared in John Ingram's *Flora Symbolica* (1869) meaning 'Love of nature, magnificence'. Its only previous appearance was in *The Catholic Language of Flowers* (1861), where it symbolized 'Lively faith'.

January 1996

Holiday, USA (Martin Luther King's birthday)

MONDAY 15

TUESDAY 16

WEDNESDAY 17

THURSDAY 18

FRIDAY 19

● SATURDAY 20

SUNDAY 21

22 MONDAY Ramadan begins (subject to sighting of moon)

23 TUESDAY RHS Flower Show

24 WEDNESDAY RHS Flower Show

25 THURSDAY

26 FRIDAY Holiday, Australia (Australia Day)

27 SATURDAY ◑

28 SUNDAY

A CULTIVAR OF

Hyacinthus orientalis

A hand-coloured stipple engraving by

PIERRE-JOSEPH REDOUTÉ from his *Choix des plus belles fleurs* (1827-33)

IN GREEK MYTHOLOGY, Hyacinthus was killed by Apollo during the course of a game. Charlotte de la Tour therefore gave the hyacinth the meaning of '*Jeu*', translated as 'Sport' or 'Games'. Thomas Miller attempted to change its meaning to 'Truth' and 'St Joseph's early life' was proposed by *The Catholic Language of Flowers* (1861), but neither proved popular. Some later publications distinguished between white hyacinths ('Unobtrusive loveliness') and purple ('Sorrowful; I am sorry').

CULTIVARS OF

Narcissus tazetta

A hand-coloured stipple engraving of tazetta daffodils by

Pierre-Joseph Redouté from his *Choix des plus belles fleurs* (1827-33)

THERE IS NO BOTANICAL DISTINCTION between a daffodil and a narcissus, and it is not always easy to tell which is meant in language of flowers books. Charlotte de la Tour gave the narcissus the meaning of '*Egoisme*' (in Greek myth, Narcissus fell in love with himself), and was followed by English writers, with such variations as 'Self-esteem' and 'Self-love'.

January/February 1996

MONDAY 29

TUESDAY 30

WEDNESDAY 31

THURSDAY 1

FRIDAY 2

SATURDAY 3

○ SUNDAY 4

5 MONDAY

6 TUESDAY   Holiday, New Zealand (Waitangi Day)

7 WEDNESDAY

8 THURSDAY

9 FRIDAY

10 SATURDAY

11 SUNDAY

Camellia 'Incarnata'

A hand-coloured line engraving by

Alfred Chandler from Chandler and Booth's

Illustrations and Descriptions of . . . the Natural Order of Camellieae (1830-31)

Camellias were generally treated as greenhouse plants in the early nineteenth century and only entered the language of flowers in the second quarter of the century, when their hardiness became apparent. Robert Tyas gave camellias the meaning of 'Unpretending excellence', a meaning later confined to red-flowered forms, while white ones came to mean 'Perfected loveliness' and, according to *The Catholic Language of Flowers* (1861), 'Chastity'.

Rosa gallica 'Maheka'

A hand-coloured stipple engraving by

PIERRE-JOSEPH REDOUTÉ from his *Les roses* (1817-24)

THE NUMBER OF MEANINGS assigned to different types of roses increased in later works on the language of flowers. John Ingram, in his *Flora Symbolica* (1869), gave 'Bashful shame' as the meaning of a deep red rose. *The Catholic Language of Flowers* (1861), attempting to lift its readers' minds to higher things, suggested 'England' as an alternative meaning.

February 1996

Holiday, USA (Lincoln's birthday)

◑ MONDAY 12

TUESDAY 13

St Valentine's Day

WEDNESDAY 14

THURSDAY 15

FRIDAY 16

SATURDAY 17

● SUNDAY 18

19 MONDAY

Holiday, USA (Washington's birthday)
Chinese New Year

20 TUESDAY

Shrove Tuesday
RHS Flower Show

21 WEDNESDAY

Ash Wednesday
RHS Flower Show

22 THURSDAY

23 FRIDAY

24 SATURDAY

25 SUNDAY

Hedera helix

A hand-coloured engraving of ivy from the second edition of

WILLIAM CURTIS's *Flora Londinensis* (1835)

'FRIENDSHIP' AND 'FIDELITY' were the most frequent meanings given for ivy. 'Marriage' was an additional meaning, and some later books specified that a sprig of ivy with tendrils meant 'Assiduous to please'.

Camellia 'Corallina'

A hand-coloured line engraving by

ALFRED CHANDLER of the camellia he raised in 1819, from Chandler and Booth's

Illustrations and Descriptions of . . . the Natural Order of Camellieae (1830-31)

ALTHOUGH VARIETIES OF YELLOW AND RED CAMELLIA were developed during the early decades of the nineteenth century, it was only in the second half of the century that the colour of camellias made a difference to their meaning in the language of flowers. The red camellia retained the original meaning for the genus, 'Unpretending excellence'. 'Beauty is your only attraction' is given in some later books as a meaning for *Camellia japonica*.

February/March 1996

◑ MONDAY 26

TUESDAY 27

WEDNESDAY 28

THURSDAY 29

St David's Day, Wales

FRIDAY 1

SATURDAY 2

SUNDAY 3

March 1996

4 MONDAY

5 TUESDAY ○

6 WEDNESDAY

7 THURSDAY

8 FRIDAY

9 SATURDAY   RHS Orchid Show

10 SUNDAY   RHS Orchid Show

Rosa pimpinellifolia inermis

A hand-coloured stipple engraving of the thornless rose by

PIERRE-JOSEPH REDOUTÉ from his *Les roses* (1817-24)

ROSES FURNISHED THE LANGUAGE OF FLOWERS with more nuances of meaning than any other plant. Even a flowerless sprig of rose was used to denote 'Separation' (Thomas Miller), and some later language of flowers books, following John Ingram's *Flora Symbolica* (1869), gave the thornless rose illustrated here as a symbol of 'Early attachment'.

CULTIVARS OF

Narcissus × *incomparabilis*

A hand-coloured stipple engraving of daffodils by

Pierre-Joseph Redouté from his *Choix des plus belles fleurs* (1827-33)

Many English writers gave different entries for daffodil and narcissus. In his *Sentiment of Flowers* (1853), Robert Tyas gave the daffodil the meaning of 'Delusive hope', because 'the flowers of this plant very often fail'. In this he was followed by other later writers, with 'Unrequited love' sometimes appearing as well. In his *Language of Flowers* (1869), Tyas added 'Disdain' as a further meaning. *The Catholic Language of Flowers* (1861) used the daffodil as a sign for 'Folly'.

Commonwealth Day

MONDAY 11

RHS Flower Show

◑ TUESDAY 12

RHS Flower Show

WEDNESDAY 13

THURSDAY 14

FRIDAY 15

SATURDAY 16

St Patrick's Day, Ireland
Mothering Sunday

SUNDAY 17

18 MONDAY   Holiday, Northern Ireland and Republic of Ireland

19 TUESDAY ●

20 WEDNESDAY   Vernal Equinox

21 THURSDAY

22 FRIDAY

23 SATURDAY

24 SUNDAY

A CULTIVAR OF

Malus sylvestris

A hand-coloured stipple engraving of the blossom of a hybrid apple by

PIERRE-JOSEPH REDOUTÉ from Duhamel du Monceau's *Traité des arbres et arbustes* (1801-25)

CHARLOTTE DE LA TOUR GAVE 'PREFERENCE' as the meaning of apple blossom, with the explanation that apple blossom might be preferred to roses. 'Preference' may be found in many English publications, but it was never a favourite meaning. The popular identification of the apple as the biblical fruit of the tree of the knowledge of good and evil led to 'Temptation' becoming more widely adopted. An additional meaning, 'Fame speaks him great and good', was also widespread.

Rosa sulfurea

A hand-coloured stipple engraving of a yellow rose by

Pierre-Joseph Redouté from his *Les roses* (1817-24)

From Charlotte de la Tour onwards, almost all language of flowers books gave the meaning of a yellow rose as 'Infidelity'. Variants from the later, more eclectic works included 'Jealousy' and 'Decrease of Love'; in some American publications these definitions apply only to the yellow sweetbriar.

MONDAY 25

TUESDAY 26

◑ WEDNESDAY 27

THURSDAY 28

FRIDAY 29

SATURDAY 30

Palm Sunday
British Summer Time begins (subject to confirmation)

SUNDAY 31

April 1996

1 MONDAY

2 TUESDAY

3 WEDNESDAY

4 THURSDAY ○   Passover (Pesach) First Day
                                                    Maundy Thursday

5 FRIDAY   Good Friday

6 SATURDAY   Holiday, Australia

7 SUNDAY   Easter Sunday

Lilium candidum

A hand-coloured stipple engraving of a Madonna lily by

P<small>IERRE</small>-J<small>OSEPH</small> R<small>EDOUTÉ</small> from his *Les liliacées* (1802-16)

C<small>HARLOTTE DE LA</small> T<small>OUR GAVE THE MEANING</small> of the white lily as 'Majesty', drawing on the French poet Boisjolin who wrote that the lily was the king of flowers, as the rose was the queen. 'Purity and modesty' were the preferred meanings in England. When other white lilies were introduced into cultivation, this lily took the name Madonna lily and was associated with 'Mary immaculate' in *The Catholic Language of Flowers* (1861).

Tulipa gesneriana

A hand-coloured stipple engraving by

PIERRE-JOSEPH REDOUTÉ from his *Choix des plus belles fleurs* (1827-33)

CHARLOTTE DE LA TOUR AND HER ENGLISH SUCCESSORS all agreed that the tulip should represent 'Declaration of love'. *The Catholic Language of Flowers* (1861) changed this to 'Presumption'. Later books gave 'Fame', originally the meaning of tulip tree, and 'Charity', originally the meaning of turnip, both perhaps originating as typographical errors. 'Beautiful eyes' was attributed to the variegated tulip and 'Hopeless love' to the yellow tulip while 'Declaration of love' was eventually restricted to the red tulip.

April 1996

Easter Monday
Holiday, UK (exc. Scotland), Republic of Ireland, Canada, Australia and New Zealand

MONDAY 8

TUESDAY 9

Passover (Pesach) Seventh Day

◑ WEDNESDAY 10

Passover (Pesach) Eighth Day

THURSDAY 11

FRIDAY 12

SATURDAY 13

SUNDAY 14

April 1996

15 MONDAY

16 TUESDAY   RHS Flower Show

17 WEDNESDAY ●   RHS Flower Show

18 THURSDAY

19 FRIDAY

20 SATURDAY

21 SUNDAY   Birthday of Queen Elizabeth II

Fritillaria imperialis

A hand-coloured stipple engraving of a crown imperial by

Pierre-Joseph Redouté from his *Choix des plus belles fleurs* (1827-33)

As its name implies, the crown imperial had been associated with imperial power since the sixteenth century, and books on the language of flowers vacillated between 'Power' and 'Majesty' as its meaning. The only minor deviation from this is found in *The Catholic Language of Flowers* (1861), where its meaning was given as 'Sovereignty'.

Iris 'Monspur'

A water-colour drawing by

Miss Williamson, made in 1905 for Ellen Willmott from a specimen in her garden at Warley Place

CHARLOTTE DE LA TOUR GAVE THE MEANING OF THE IRIS as 'Message', drawing an analogy between the many colours of iris varieties and the rainbow which was God's message to mankind. De la Tour's meaning was universally followed. Even *The Catholic Language of Flowers* (1861) went no further than to specify its meaning as 'Messages from heaven'.

MONDAY 22

St George's Day, England

TUESDAY 23

WEDNESDAY 24

Holiday, Australia and New Zealand (Anzac Day)
Harrogate Spring Show

◐ THURSDAY 25

Harrogate Spring Show

FRIDAY 26

Harrogate Spring Show

SATURDAY 27

Harrogate Spring Show

SUNDAY 28

---

29 MONDAY

30 TUESDAY   RHS Flower Show

1 WEDNESDAY   RHS Flower Show

2 THURSDAY

3 FRIDAY ○

4 SATURDAY

5 SUNDAY

Convallaria majalis

A hand-coloured stipple engraving of lily of the valley by

Pierre-Joseph Redouté from his *Les liliacées* (1802-16)

Virtually every language of flowers book gave 'Return of happiness' as the meaning for the lily of the valley. The only exception, as so often, was *The Catholic Language of Flowers* (1861), which redefined it as 'Reserve'. In some later books the additional meaning 'Unconscious sweetness' was given.

Wisteria sinensis

A chromolithograph of the drawing by

A. J. WENDEL from Hendrik Witte's *Flora* (1868)

THE WISTERIA WAS A LATE ADDITION to the language of flowers books, first appearing in the 1860s when it became popular as an open-air climber (having previously been treated as a greenhouse plant). The later books gave its meaning as 'Welcome, fair stranger'.

May 1996

May Day Holiday, UK (exc. Scotland) and Republic of Ireland
Spring Holiday, Scotland

MONDAY 6

TUESDAY 7

WEDNESDAY 8

THURSDAY 9

Malvern Spring Gardening Show

◖ FRIDAY 10

Malvern Spring Gardening Show

SATURDAY 11

Mother's Day, Canada and USA
Malvern Spring Gardening Show

SUNDAY 12

May 1996

13 MONDAY

14 TUESDAY

15 WEDNESDAY

16 THURSDAY   Ascension Day

17 FRIDAY ●

18 SATURDAY

19 SUNDAY   Islamic New Year (subject to sighting of moon)

A Noisette rose

A hand-coloured stipple engraving by

PIERRE-JOSEPH REDOUTÉ from his *Les roses* (1817-24)

CHARLOTTE DE LA TOUR CHOSE ROSEBUDS to signify a young girl, and in this she was followed by the English writers. In the second half of the nineteenth century, some books distinguished between white rosebuds ('Girlhood'), red rosebuds ('Pure and lovely') and moss rosebuds ('Confession of love'), this latter meaning derived from Thomas Miller's *Poetical Language of Flowers* (1847).

Polygonatum multiflorum

A hand-coloured stipple engraving of Solomon's seal by

Pierre-Joseph Redouté from his *Les liliacées* (1802-16)

Called 'Our Lady's seal' in medieval times, polygonatum was renamed after the Protestant Reformation, in order to avoid associations with the Virgin Mary, and became known as Solomon's seal. Possibly because of its continuing, if transformed, religious associations, the language of flowers overlooked this plant. For the same reason, however, *The Catholic Language of Flowers* (1861) found a place for it, representing 'Wisdom'.

May 1996

Holiday, Canada (Victoria Day)

MONDAY 20

Chelsea Flower Show

TUESDAY 21

Chelsea Flower Show

WEDNESDAY 22

Chelsea Flower Show

THURSDAY 23

Jewish Feast of weeks (Shavuot)
Chelsea Flower Show

FRIDAY 24

◑ SATURDAY 25

Whit Sunday (Pentecost)

SUNDAY 26

May/June 1996

WEEK 22

27 MONDAY

Spring Holiday, UK (exc. Scotland)
May Day Holiday, Scotland
Holiday, USA (Memorial Day)

28 TUESDAY

29 WEDNESDAY

30 THURSDAY

31 FRIDAY

1 SATURDAY ○

2 SUNDAY

Trinity Sunday

Lathyrus odoratus

A hand-coloured stipple engraving of sweet peas by

PIERRE-JOSEPH REDOUTÉ from his *Choix des plus belles fleurs* (1827-33)

THE SWEET PEA WAS INTRODUCED into cultivation in Europe in the early eighteenth century. The flower's popularity grew during the nineteenth century, but it only became fashionable in the Edwardian period. Thomas Miller's *Poetical Language of Flowers* (1847) was the first book to list an interpretation of the sweet pea: here it stood simply for 'Pleasure'. From the 1840s most books expanded on Miller, giving 'Delicate pleasure' and 'Departure' as alternative meanings.

Rosa damascena

A hand-coloured stipple engraving of a Damask rose by

PIERRE-JOSEPH REDOUTÉ from his *Les roses* (1817-24)

CHARLOTTE DE LA TOUR and her English follower Robert Tyas gave the meaning of the Damask rose as 'Beauty ever new'. This seems not to have been specific enough for the needs of English writers, for it is more common to find 'Freshness of complexion' or, later, 'Brilliant complexion' given instead. *The Catholic Language of Flowers* (1861) redefined it as 'Beneficence'.

Holiday, Republic of Ireland
Holiday, New Zealand (Queen's Birthday)

MONDAY 3

TUESDAY 4

WEDNESDAY 5

Corpus Christi

THURSDAY 6

FRIDAY 7

The Queen's Official Birthday (subject to confirmation)

◑ SATURDAY 8

SUNDAY 9

10 MONDAY   Holiday, Australia (Queen's Birthday)

11 TUESDAY

12 WEDNESDAY

13 THURSDAY

14 FRIDAY

15 SATURDAY

16 SUNDAY ●   Father's Day, UK, Canada and USA

Papaver somniferum

A hand-coloured stipple engraving of poppies by

PIERRE-JOSEPH REDOUTÉ from his *Choix des plus belles fleurs* (1827-33)

CHARLOTTE DE LA TOUR GAVE THE MEANING of the white poppy as 'Sleep of the heart' and the red poppy 'Consolation' (a meaning shared with the snowdrop). English writers wrestled with the contradiction between this and the traditional association of poppies with sleep. As a result, poppies came to mean both 'Oblivion' and 'Consolation to the sick'; and some works listed 'Fantastic extravagance' as an extra meaning for the scarlet poppy.

Paeonia lactiflora

A hand-coloured stipple engraving by

Pierre-Joseph Redouté from his *Choix des plus belles fleurs* (1827-33)

The seventeenth-century poet René Rapin had characterized the peony as the flower of shame:
Whose Blushes might the Praise of Virture claim,
But her vile Scent betrays they rise from shame . . .
For this reason Charlotte de la Tour and her English followers gave the meaning of the peony as 'Shame', although some later publications altered this to 'Bashfulness'.

June 1996

MONDAY 17

TUESDAY 18

WEDNESDAY 19

THURSDAY 20

Summer Solstice

FRIDAY 21

SATURDAY 22

SUNDAY 23

June 1996

24 MONDAY ◑

---

25 TUESDAY   RHS Flower Show

---

26 WEDNESDAY   RHS Flower Show

---

27 THURSDAY

---

28 FRIDAY   Wisley Flower Show

---

29 SATURDAY   Wisley Flower Show

---

30 SUNDAY

Syringa vulgaris

A hand-coloured stipple engraving of lilac by

PIERRE-JOSEPH REDOUTÉ from his *Choix des plus belles fleurs* (1827-33)

BECAUSE IT FLOWERED EARLY IN THE SEASON, Charlotte de la Tour chose the lilac to signify 'First emotions of love', and was followed in this by most English writers. A few works gave 'Forsaken', which was more usually the meaning ascribed to the anemone. *The Catholic Language of Flowers* (1861) redefined lilac as meaning 'Meekness'.

A VARIETY OF

Rosa gallica

A hand-coloured stipple engraving by

PIERRE-JOSEPH REDOUTÉ from his *Les roses* (1817-24)

Roses had many subtleties of meaning in the language of flowers. As early as 1818, Charlotte de la Tour gave distinct meanings for a rose leaf ('I never importune') and a rose presented in a tuft of grass ('There is everything to be gained by good company'). In some later books, a full-blown rose placed over two buds in a bouquet was used to indicate 'Secrecy'.

July 1996

Holiday, Canada (Canada Day)

○ MONDAY 1

TUESDAY 2

WEDNESDAY 3

Holiday, USA (Independence Day)

THURSDAY 4

FRIDAY 5

SATURDAY 6

◑ SUNDAY 7

8 MONDAY

---

9 TUESDAY · Hampton Court Palace Flower Show

---

10 WEDNESDAY · Hampton Court Palace Flower Show

---

11 THURSDAY · Hampton Court Palace Flower Show

---

12 FRIDAY · Holiday, Northern Ireland (Battle of the Boyne)
Hampton Court Palace Flower Show

---

13 SATURDAY · Hampton Court Palace Flower Show

---

14 SUNDAY · Hampton Court Palace Flower Show

Aesculus hippocastanum

A hand-coloured stipple engraving of horse chestnut by

PIERRE-JOSEPH REDOUTÉ from Duhamel du Monceau's *Traité des arbres et arbustes* (1801-25)

WHEN THE LANGUAGE OF FLOWERS WAS DEVELOPING, the horse chestnut was a rich man's tree, charac-terized by Charlotte de la Tour as astonishing the vulgar with its useless luxury – useless because its fruits were inedible. 'Luxury' therefore remained its meaning, except in *The Catholic Language of Flowers* (1861) where it was used to mean 'Fraternal affection'.

Antirrhinum majus

A hand-coloured stipple engraving of a snapdragon by

PIERRE-JOSEPH REDOUTÉ from his *Choix des plus belles fleurs* (1827-33)

CHARLOTTE DE LA TOUR AND THE EARLIER ENGLISH WRITERS on the language of flowers gave the meaning of the snapdragon as 'Presumption'. In his *Poetical Language of Flowers* (1847), Thomas Miller concocted the alternative meaning of 'Refusal' and this appears in some later works, one American book abridging its meaning simply to 'No'.

July 1996

St Swithin's Day

● MONDAY 15

TUESDAY 16

WEDNESDAY 17

THURSDAY 18

FRIDAY 19

SATURDAY 20

SUNDAY 21

July 1996

22 MONDAY

23 TUESDAY ◑   RHS Flower Show

24 WEDNESDAY   RHS Flower Show

25 THURSDAY

26 FRIDAY

27 SATURDAY

28 SUNDAY

Lonicera caprifolium

A hand-coloured stipple engraving of honeysuckle by

PIERRE-JOSEPH REDOUTÉ from his *Choix des plus belles fleurs* (1827-33)

'BONDS OF LOVE' was given as the meaning of the honeysuckle by Charlotte de la Tour and most of her English successors. Thomas Miller's *Poetical Language of Flowers* (1847) attempted to replace this by 'Devoted affection' and this meaning was picked up by some of the later works. 'Sweetness of disposition' was an additional meaning which appeared in most English works, later augmented in American publications as 'Generous and devoted affection'.

A FORM OF

Robinia hispida

A hand-coloured stipple engraving of rose acacia by

PIERRE-JOSEPH REDOUTÉ from Duhamel du Monceau's *Traité des arbres et arbustes* (1801-25)

CHARLOTTE DE LA TOUR USED THE ROSE ACACIA (*Robinia hispida*) to mean 'Elegance' and the common acacia' (*Robinia pseudoacacia*) to mean 'Platonic love'. This latter meaning was rephrased by most of her English followers as 'Chaste love' or, later, 'Friendship'.

July/August 1996

MONDAY 29

○ TUESDAY 30

WEDNESDAY 31

THURSDAY 1

FRIDAY 2

SATURDAY 3

SUNDAY 4

August 1996

5 MONDAY

6 TUESDAY ◐

7 WEDNESDAY

8 THURSDAY

9 FRIDAY

10 SATURDAY

11 SUNDAY

Ipomoea quamoclit

A hand-coloured stipple engraving of a morning glory by

PIERRE-JOSEPH REDOUTÉ from his *Choix des plus belles fleurs* (1827-33)

PREDICTABLY FOR A CLINGING PLANT, the ipomoea was used by Charlotte de la Tour and her English followers to mean 'I attach myself to you'. This was later to become merely 'Attachment' and was sometimes reserved for red-flowered species, while others were given the meaning 'Affectation'.

Passiflora caerulea

A hand-coloured stipple engraving of a passion flower by

Mary Lawrance from her *A Collection of Passion Flowers coloured from Nature* (1799-1802)

THE PASSION FLOWER HAD BEEN SO CALLED since the sixteenth century because its unusual floral struc-
ture gave rise to analogies with the passion of Christ. French books on the language of flowers therefore gave its meaning as 'Faith'; Protestant English authors, however, were suspicious of this meaning
and usually substituted 'Superstition'.

August 1996

MONDAY 12

TUESDAY 13

● WEDNESDAY 14

THURSDAY 15

FRIDAY 16

SATURDAY 17

SUNDAY 18

19 MONDAY

20 TUESDAY   RHS Flower Show

21 WEDNESDAY   RHS Flower Show

22 THURSDAY ◐

23 FRIDAY

24 SATURDAY

25 SUNDAY

Iris × monnieri

A water-colour drawing by

Miss Williamson, made in 1905 for Ellen Willmott from a specimen in her garden at Warley Place

Flamme or Flambe was a French vernacular name for the yellow iris; Charlotte de la Tour, in making 'Flame' its meaning in the language of flowers, was simply adopting a common convention. English writers tried to find interpretations that would justify the meaning, and so 'Ardour' and 'Flame of Love' will often be found in English language of flowers books.

Clematis viticella

A hand-coloured stipple engraving by

PIERRE-JOSEPH REDOUTÉ from Duhamel du Monceau's *Traité des arbres et arbustes* (1801-25)

CLEMATIS HAD TWO CONTRASTING MEANINGS in the language of flowers. The earlier meaning, given by Charlotte de la Tour, was 'artifice', derived from beggars' use of clematis leaves to produce skin ulcers so as to excite pity. The young George Eliot was nicknamed 'Clematis' because of the plant's alternative meaning, 'Mental beauty'.

August/September 1996

Summer Holiday, UK (exc. Scotland)

MONDAY 26

TUESDAY 27

○ WEDNESDAY 28

THURSDAY 29

FRIDAY 30

SATURDAY 31

SUNDAY 1

September 1996

2 MONDAY   Holiday, Canada (Labour Day) and USA (Labor Day)

3 TUESDAY

4 WEDNESDAY ◑

5 THURSDAY

6 FRIDAY

7 SATURDAY

8 SUNDAY

Tropaeolum majus

A hand-coloured stipple engraving of a nasturtium by

PIERRE-JOSEPH REDOUTÉ from his *Choix des plus belles fleurs* (1827-33)

ENGLISH PLANT BREEDERS IN THE EARLY NINETEENTH CENTURY frequently gave their flowers military names: auriculas, polyanthus and pinks bore titles like 'Defiance', 'Britannia' and 'Hertfordshire Hero'. In his *Sentiment of Flowers* (1853), Robert Tyas gave 'Patriotism' as the nasturtium's meaning. *The Catholic Language of Flowers* (1861), perhaps responding to this definition, redefined it as 'The applause of the world'.

A FORM OF

Rosa alba

A hand-coloured stipple engraving by

PIERRE-JOSEPH REDOUTÉ from his *Les roses* (1817-24)

CHARLOTTE DE LA TOUR and most of her English followers gave the meaning of the white rose as 'Silence', from its association with the classical god of silence. Some later works changed this to 'I am worthy of you', while specifying that a withered white rose meant 'Transient impressions', and a dried one, 'Death is preferable to loss of innocence'.

September 1996

MONDAY 9

TUESDAY 10

WEDNESDAY 11

● THURSDAY 12

Harrogate Great Autumn Show

FRIDAY 13

Jewish New Year (Rosh Hashanah)
Harrogate Great Autumn Show

SATURDAY 14

Harrogate Great Autumn Show

SUNDAY 15

16 MONDAY

17 TUESDAY   RHS Great Autumn Show

18 WEDNESDAY   RHS Great Autumn Show

19 THURSDAY

20 FRIDAY ◑

21 SATURDAY   Malvern Autumn Show

22 SUNDAY   Autumnal Equinox
           Malvern Autumn Show

Nerium oleander

A hand-coloured stipple engraving of oleander by

<small>PIERRE-JOSEPH REDOUTÉ</small> from his *Choix des plus belles fleurs* (1827-33)

OLEANDER HAS A LONG HISTORY IN EUROPE, being known in the Mediterranean from classical times and grown in England from the sixteenth century. Nevertheless, it entered the language of flowers late, and is not to be found until the middle of the nineteenth century, when its meaning is given as 'Beware', possibly because, although used medicinally in mild doses, most of its parts are poisonous.

Lilium bulbiferum

A hand-coloured stipple engraving by

Pierre-Joseph Redouté from his *Les liliacées* (1802-16)

Lilies of colours other than white were late additions to the language of flowers. In 1861, *The Catholic Language of Flowers* gave 'A passionate disposition' as the meaning for orange lilies, while later American books identified yellow lilies with 'Falsehood, gaiety'.

September 1996

Jewish Day of Atonement (Yom Kippur)

MONDAY 23

TUESDAY 24

WEDNESDAY 25

THURSDAY 26

○ FRIDAY 27

Jewish Festival of Tabernacles (Succoth) First Day

SATURDAY 28

Michaelmas Day

SUNDAY 29

September/October 1996

30 MONDAY

1 TUESDAY

2 WEDNESDAY

3 THURSDAY

4 FRIDAY ◐

5 SATURDAY   Jewish Festival of Tabernacles (Succoth) Eighth Day

6 SUNDAY

Jasminum grandiflorum

A hand-coloured stipple engraving of Spanish jasmine by

Pierre-Joseph Redouté from his *Choix des plus belles fleurs* (1827-33)

THE COMMON JASMINE, *Jasminum officinale*, was used by Charlotte de la Tour and her English follow-ers to stand for 'Amiableness' or 'Amiability'. The Spanish jasmine shown here, although well known in gardens in de la Tour's time, did not enter the language of flowers until the second half of the nine-teenth century, when it came to stand for 'Sensuality'.

Asphodelus lutea

A hand-coloured stipple engraving of asphodel by

Pierre-Joseph Redouté from his *Les liliacées* (1802-16)

ASPHODEL WAS A PLANT WITH STRONG CLASSICAL ASSOCIATIONS known to have been used as a funeral decoration, and it was universally adopted to mean 'My regrets follow you to the grave'. Thomas Miller, in his *Poetical Language of Flowers* (1847), altered this slightly to 'Regret and sorrow for the dead'.

MONDAY 7

RHS Flower Show

TUESDAY 8

RHS Flower Show

WEDNESDAY 9

THURSDAY 10

FRIDAY 11

● SATURDAY 12

SUNDAY 13

October 1996

14 MONDAY   Holiday, Canada (Thanksgiving) and USA (Columbus Day)

---

15 TUESDAY

---

16 WEDNESDAY

---

17 THURSDAY

---

18 FRIDAY

---

19 SATURDAY ◑

---

20 SUNDAY

Rosa muscosa

A hand-coloured stipple engraving of the moss rose by

Pierre-Joseph Redouté from his *Les roses* (1817-24)

Charlotte de la Tour gave 'Love, voluptuousness' as the meanings of the moss rose, but many English books chastened its meaning to 'Pleasure without alloy', and *The Catholic Language of Flowers* (1861) used it to mean 'Holiness'. A moss rosebud, following Thomas Miller, was used to mean 'Confession of love'.

Dendranthema indicum

A hand-coloured stipple engraving of chrysanthemum by

PIERRE-JOSEPH REDOUTÉ from his *Choix des plus belles fleurs* (1827-33)

IN HIS *SENTIMENT OF FLOWERS* (1853), Robert Tyas offered 'Cheerfulness in adversity' as the meaning of the chrysanthemum, because it extended the flowering season into the autumn, a formerly bleak time in the flower garden. A similar association with autumn led *The Catholic Language of Flowers* (1861) to redefine it as 'Farewell'. As the varieties of chrysanthemum multiplied, so did their meanings in the language of flowers: red chrysanthemums came to signify 'I love', white to mean 'Truth', and yellow to stand for 'Slighted love'.

October 1996

MONDAY 21

TUESDAY 22

WEDNESDAY 23

United Nations Day

THURSDAY 24

FRIDAY 25

○ SATURDAY 26

British Summer Time ends (subject to confirmation)

SUNDAY 27

October/November 1996

28 MONDAY

Holiday, Republic of Ireland
Holiday, New Zealand (Labour Day)

29 TUESDAY

30 WEDNESDAY

31 THURSDAY

Hallowe'en

1 FRIDAY

All Saints' Day

2 SATURDAY

3 SUNDAY ◑

An early double dahlia

A hand-coloured stipple engraving by

PIERRE-JOSEPH REDOUTÉ from his *Choix des plus belles fleurs* (1827-33)

ACCORDING TO CHARLOTTE DE LA TOUR, a bouquet of dahlias signified '*Ma reconnaissance compasse vos soins*', but the only English writer to follow her in this definition was Robert Tyas in his *Language of Flowers* (1869): 'My gratitude exceeds your care'. Most English writers, including Tyas himself in earlier years, gave 'Instability' as the plant's meaning. *The Catholic Language of Flowers* (1861) re-defined it as 'Ornament'.

A CULTIVAR OF

Hydrangea macrophylla

A hand-coloured stipple engraving by

Pierre-Joseph Redouté from his *Choix des plus belles fleurs* (1827-33)

Charlotte de la Tour used the hydrangea to convey the message *'Vous êtes froide'*, but the early English books changed this to 'Boaster'. Some American writers, however, gave entries for both hydrangea and hortensia, possibly unaware that both names referred to the same plant, and gave 'You are cold' as the meaning for the latter.

MONDAY 4

Guy Fawkes' Day
RHS Flower Show

TUESDAY 5

RHS Flower Show

WEDNESDAY 6

THURSDAY 7

FRIDAY 8

SATURDAY 9

Remembrance Sunday

SUNDAY 10

11 MONDAY ●   Holiday, Canada (Remembrance Day) and USA (Veterans' Day)

12 TUESDAY

13 WEDNESDAY

14 THURSDAY

15 FRIDAY

16 SATURDAY

17 SUNDAY

Rosa centifolia

A hand-coloured stipple engraving by

PIERRE-JOSEPH REDOUTÉ from his *Les roses* (1817-24)

CHARLOTTE DE LA TOUR GAVE THE MEANING OF THIS ROSE as 'The Graces'. Most early language of flowers books, missing the classical allusion, modified this to 'Graces'. In some later books the meaning was changed to 'Pride' or 'Dignity of mind', and 'Grace' was given as the meaning of the Multiflora rose instead.

Gladiolus undulatus

A hand-coloured stipple engraving by

PIERRE-JOSEPH REDOUTÉ from his *Les liliacées* (1802-16)

THE GLADIOLUS WAS A SUBJECT of experimental plant breeding during the early nineteenth century but had to wait until late in the century before it became the popular flower it is today. Consequently it does not appear in the early books on the language of flowers. John Ingram, in his *Flora Symbolica* (1869), gives its meaning as 'Ready armed', drawing on its etymology (gladiolus = little sword).

November 1996

◑ MONDAY 18

TUESDAY 19

WEDNESDAY 20

THURSDAY 21

FRIDAY 22

SATURDAY 23

SUNDAY 24

25 MONDAY ○

26 TUESDAY

RHS Flower Show

27 WEDNESDAY

RHS Flower Show

28 THURSDAY

Holiday, USA (Thanksgiving Day)

29 FRIDAY

30 SATURDAY

St Andrew's Day, Scotland

1 SUNDAY

Advent Sunday

Viola tricolor

A hand-coloured stipple engraving of heartsease pansies by

Pierre-Joseph Redouté from his *Choix des plus belles fleurs* (1827-33)

HEARTSEASE PANSIES, as shown in Redouté's illustration, had the traditional meaning of 'Thought' (from the French *pensée*). When the modern pansy (cultivars of *Viola* × *wittrockiana*) was developed in about 1840, writers on the language of flowers kept 'Thought' as the meaning for both the old and the new plants. Some books offered slight variations such as 'You occupy my thoughts'.

Anemone coronaria

A hand-coloured stipple engraving by

PIERRE-JOSEPH REDOUTÉ from his *Choix des plus belles fleurs* (1827-33)

CHARLOTTE DE LA TOUR GAVE 'ABANDON' as the meaning for the anemone, because in Greek mythology the nymph Anemone had been abandoned by her lover Zephyr. English writers translated this as 'Forsaken'. *The Catholic Language of Flowers* (1861) adapted this meaning slightly to 'Jesus forsaken'.

December 1996

MONDAY 2

◑ TUESDAY 3

WEDNESDAY 4

THURSDAY 5

Jewish Festival of Chanukah, First Day
FRIDAY 6

SATURDAY 7

SUNDAY 8

December 1996

9 MONDAY

---

10 TUESDAY ●   RHS Christmas Show

---

11 WEDNESDAY   RHS Christmas Show

---

12 THURSDAY

---

13 FRIDAY   Jewish Festival of Chanukah, Eighth Day

---

14 SATURDAY

---

15 SUNDAY

Digitalis purpurea

A hand-coloured stipple engraving of a common foxglove by

Ferdinand Bauer from John Lindley's *Digitalium Monographia* (1821)

In medieval times this plant was variously called 'Foxglove' and 'Our Lady's gloves'. After the Protestant Reformation, when associations with the Virgin Mary were discouraged in plant names, 'Foxglove' completely displaced its rival name. Not all language of flowers books included it, but those that did, including *The Catholic Language of Flowers* (1861), gave its meaning as 'Insincerity'.

Acanthus mollis

A hand-coloured stipple engraving of acanthus by

Ferdinand Bauer from John Sibthorp's *Flora Graeca* (1806-40)

THE ACANTHUS, ACCORDING TO CLASSICAL TRADITION, was the model for the decoration of the Corinthian capital, and so it was appropriated as a symbol of the arts. That remained its meaning in the language of flowers until later books, perhaps through a misunderstanding, altered this to 'Artifice'.

December 1996

MONDAY 16

◑ TUESDAY 17

WEDNESDAY 18

THURSDAY 19

FRIDAY 20

Winter Solstice

SATURDAY 21

SUNDAY 22

23 MONDAY

24 TUESDAY ○   Christmas Eve

25 WEDNESDAY
Christmas Day
Holiday, UK, Republic of Ireland, Canada, USA, Australia and New Zealand

26 THURSDAY
Boxing Day, St Stephen's Day
Holiday, UK, Republic of Ireland, Canada, Australia and New Zealand

27 FRIDAY

28 SATURDAY

29 SUNDAY

An amaryllis or hippeastrum

A hand-coloured stipple engraving by

PIERRE-JOSEPH REDOUTÉ from his *Les liliacées* (1802-16)

WHEN IS AN AMARYLLIS NOT AN AMARYLLIS? Charlotte de la Tour reported that gardeners called it a proud plant, because it often refused to flower when they wanted, and she therefore made it a symbol of pride. But her 'amaryllis' included the Guernsey lily (*Nerine sarniensis*) as well as the plant now known as hippeastrum. In language of flowers books, 'Haughtiness' and 'Pride' remained the standard meanings of this group of plants, although, perversely, 'Timidity' was given as the meaning in an American work.

Myosotis scorpioides

A hand-coloured stipple engraving of a forget-me-not by

PIERRE-JOSEPH REDOUTÉ from his *Choix des plus belles fleurs* (1827-33)

IN THE SIXTEENTH CENTURY, the myosotis was apparently used as a lovers' charm; its French name, *'ne m'oubliez pas'*, was translated to form its common names in German and English. Accordingly 'Forget me not' became its standard meaning in the language of flowers. Some works gave 'True love' as an additional meaning.

December 1996/*January* 1997

MONDAY 30

TUESDAY 31

New Year's Day
Holiday, UK, Republic of Ireland, Canada, USA, Australia and New Zealand

WEDNESDAY 1

Holiday, Scotland and New Zealand

◐ THURSDAY 2

FRIDAY 3

SATURDAY 4

SUNDAY 5

EUROPEAN NATIONAL HOLIDAYS 1996

Holidays that fall on a Sunday are not included

AUSTRIA	January 1, 6; April 8; May 1, 16, 27; June 6; August 15; October 26; November 1; December 25, 26
BELGIUM	January 1; April 8; May 1, 16, 27; August 15; November 1, 11; December 25
DENMARK	January 1; April 4, 5, 8; May 3, 16, 27; June 5; December 24, 25, 26
FINLAND	January 1, 6; April 5, 8; May 1, 16; June 22; November 2; December 6, 25, 26
FRANCE	January 1; April 8; May 1, 8, 16, 27; August 15; November 1, 11; December 25
GERMANY	January 1; April 5, 8; May 1, 16, 27; October 3; December 25, 26
GREECE	January 1, 6; March 25; April 12, 15; May 1; June 3; August 15; October 28; December 25, 26
ITALY	January 1, 6; April 8, 25; May 1; August 15; November 1; December 25, 26
LUXEMBOURG	January 1; April 8; May 1, 16, 27; August 15; November 1, 2; December 25, 26
NETHERLANDS	January 1; April 8, 30; May 16, 27; December 25, 26
NORWAY	January 1; April 4, 5, 8; May 1, 16, 17, 27; December 25, 26
PORTUGAL	January 1; April 5, 25; May 1; June 6, 10; August 15; October 5; November 1; December 25
SPAIN	January 1, 6; April 5; May 1; August 15; October 12; November 1; December 6, 25
SWEDEN	January 1, 6; April 5, 8; May 1, 16, 27; June 22; November 2; December 25, 26
SWITZERLAND	January 1; April 5, 8; May 1, 16, 27; August 1; December 25, 26